VANISHING POINT

Colin Bancroft has a PhD on the Ecopoetics Robert Frost. His pamphlet *Impermanence* was released with Maytree Press in 2020 and *Kayfabe* with Legitimate Snack in 2021. His pamphlet *Knife Edge* (Broken Sleep Books) was released in April 2022. He is editor at *Nine Pens Press* and runs the Poets' Directory.

Also by Colin Bancroft

CONTENTS

For Idris

ISBN: 978-1-916938-76-2

Cover designed by Aaron Kent

Cover Image: © Rob Thorley / Adobe Stock

Edited and Typeset by Aaron Kent

Broken Sleep Books Ltd
PO BOX 102
Llandysul
SA44 9BG

Vanishing Point

Colin Bancroft

Broken Sleep Books

BOTANICAL NOTES:

Eight foot tall by the garden gate:
cheerleaders at the top of their game.

The bees' electric crackles their blue air,
a storm front of ball lightning.

For weeks they will be a solar system
of planets, big gas giants bloating

in the late summer sun, swirling
in their unspectral atmospheres

as they begin to go dark,
and collapse in on themselves like stars.

                  *

A cluster of cirrus cupped floret suns
disked at different heights to catch what little

light leaks down to their sequestered nook
of gravel, broken bricks and sand.

There seems to be little for them here,
but the rhizome must run deep

to some rich resource because here they are,
blooming boldly, spreading wide,

putting down roots in the most unlikely place,
declaring this their own little corner of home.

                    *

Why are these little white lampshades the first
to break through the litter by the hawthorn hedge.

What ministry has compelled their crusade
to be the vanguard through the frozen crust.

They are the heraldry of thaw,
the liminal leakage of some vast subterranean

tabula rasa priming the underworld
in readiness for the release of colour.

Look, the daffodil's candle is rising from its bulb
to burst-blaze in undiminished wattage.

DEVELOPMENTS

I always stopped to listen to bird song
from the copse of oak beyond the lane.
No two concerts were ever the same.
But now the trees are long
gone. Now there are houses, and cars
that bang out drum n bass and old-skool
hip-hop – a forest of streetlamps that spool
out their clutter to efface the stars.

CUBBINGTON PEAR

It was a few months before it was felled
that I was out on the edge of that field.
From a distance its blossom
was seemingly suspended in the air,
like a plume of smoke stopped mid-frame.
I'd read all about it: Tree of the Year,
a national champion that couldn't be saved
because its trunk was as hollow as a tunnel.
Yet it still bore fruit right up to this last
of its two hundred and fifty summers.
I snapped a few shots, sat for a while in its shadow,
listened to the ticking engine of a blackbird
buried somewhere deep in the foliage.
Then it began to rain, the sky grew darker,
I flicked up my hood and pulled up the zip,
a train track running past my heart
right through the green fabric of my parka.

BATTLEFIELD
Shrewsbury 1403

It could have been a day just like this
                when it all kicked off:
Henry off to quash a Welsh rebellion,
Hotspur sensing his chance for glory.
Both converging upon this place
And both ending the day
                With an arrow in their face.
I bet not much has changed:
The hawthorn hedge in full flower,
The hazy heat, the lowing of a bull
And the milestone, a white shield in the sun,
Weather-rounded and smooth, like a skull.

STANDING

The gate post boulder had stood
sentry for centuries by the entrance
to the field until, forced to yield
by rain, its foundations washed away,
teetering on tiptoes, balancing on a perilous
pivot, the farmer came and attached chains
to his tractor and extracted it like a tooth
from the gummy earth. Now it lays in the grass:
a fallen shield, a medieval casket, a basking seal.
Lambs will use it as a climbing frame,
lichens will decorate, mosses baize,
and it will see out the counting of days
sinking back into England, then beyond.

LUMB

Limbless it rises through the woodland
half-dressed in its skirt of sycamore and oak,
warmed now only by the morning sun
that has bleached its blackened bricks.
A new workforce of buttercups, campion
and nettles crowd its base, birdsong replacing
the grind and hammer of industry.
Everything swallowed up by time
except the desire lines that run through the scrub,
made by those who come to touch
this obelisk, monument, minaret, lumb;
a smokeless stack that from this angle seems
to pump out clouds and clouds of green,
filling the whole valley with trees.

SIKE HEAD

'There I dropped pebbles, listened, heard
The reservoir of darkness stirred'
  — W H Auden

He would have come to see

the ramshackle ruins at Shildon

when he turned up that Easter,

to knock back champagne

and play honky-tonk at the Crewe.

Perhaps he also retraced that childhood trek

over the moor from Rookhope

to the ruined chimneys

at Sike Head, where he kicked

through the waste, looking for a trace

of galena, chalcedony,

and finding instead that shaft -

the one now covered by the grill

where we stood last summer

watching the lapwings taper –

that for him would have been a gaping

hole, a passage into himself,

into something so deeply ingrained

that he couldn't explain,

but something he'd use, mine,

tap like a vein.

OUT FOR STARS

A midwinter night and we were out on the moor
making our way along the incline path.
Once a railway ran up here hauling lead,
iron ore and limestone down the half-mile
track to Rookhope in the valley.
Now there is nothing but heather and moss,
shooting butts and the abandoned farmhouse.
And not even these existed in that darkness,
only our footsteps and the drunken swing
of the torchlight beyond our feet.
We were miners in that blackness,
forging through some underground vault,
surfacing from the depths to see the moon
crest the hill, blazing like the headlamp
of a train that surely would not stop in time.

THE LAW

Possession is 9/10ths and today it's mine.
The cartway is fortified with spoils
of pink fluorite, curved crystal calcites.
In the distance the cairn shimmers in the haze.
A football pitch of sphagnum moss
borders a drainage grip full of dark water,
nothing ripples the surface. Match abandoned.
The ruins of the lead mine seem a starkness,
lunar, rubble strewn, pock marked pit craters
mark the entrances to caved in shafts.
A capstan winch rusts on top of the level.
The chimney of the smelting mill left
as a monument to industry long gone.
Nothing can live in this place, sanitised,
ripped up, torn apart, a bombed-out battleground.
Then a rabbit bolts for its hole in the spoil.
A grouse races out of the heather
like a motorbike and a desert of lapwings,
their calls a penny arcade, tilt upwards
towards the sun and I forget the men
who worked here, and all the damage done,
and realise the fight is over, the Law had won.

THE MAP IS NOT THE TERRITORY

This hill is nothing like the sheet.
Nothing is flat, silent, static.
The land rises and falls like the sea
and is as vast and dark and ambivalent.
The paper carries with it none of the colour
of the purple heather or the clay pools
on the track that look like vats of tea.
The page brings nothing to bear of the sky,
hammered over us like a tin roof,
rattling with rain, lifted and wind-thrown.
The map knows nothing of animals,
the oystercatchers frantic circling beep,
or the spluttering engine of the grouse,
nor the bleached skull of a sheep
left as totem on the dry-stone wall.
And so, it is for all of the places
we inhabit, the map is not the territory:
not Time, nor history, not even the body
with its othered curves and dips,
strange colours and noise. So familiar
in its state of skin-deep symbolism
that we forget about the unseen world below

where fear or cancer or love
is all going on, is beginning to grow.

REWILD

I stepped across the broken stile
and took the old plantation path
through where the forestry workers had
cleared a square of half a mile.
Already grass had begun to grow
around the stumps of fallen trees,
nettles with their spiky greaves
were new defences, thickly sown.
And in the middle of the track
a single beech (a decade old?)
was a standard planted bold
as if to say *we're taking back*
this land that is our land by right:
come at us then, with all your might,
we won't go down without a fight.

LAMPING

A winter's night and out in the field
a light flared incandescently.
Minutes passed. Then again. Dazzlingly.
Cutting a corridor across the pasture
down which a lurcher, owl-white,
tore after a rabbit's shade.
Again, and again, the apparition appeared,
conjured from nothingness,
a banking, twisting, ephemeral wraith.
Momentary. Fragmentary.
Then gone in a flash over the hill,
leaving nothing but the expectant dark
and the corpse candle moon
guttering over the fell.

BETWEEN LITTLE AND GREAT DUN FELL

A spine of stone stretches across the boggy col,
Each slab reclaimed from fallen northern mills.
Two hundred years ago these blocks were floors
in dark and dusty rooms where workers stood
for hours on end feeding threads into a loom.
They had no thought for these high moors,
Gore-Tex, Go-Pro's, Open Access Rights,
for them outdoors was a dark walk home,
a Sunday trudge to church, not hikes
up to a radar dome and lunch beneath a currick.
Now these steps that line the ridge like unmarked
graves are all that's left of that dimming past,
unless you count the clumps of cotton grass
ghosting up along the edges of the path.

SPATE IN THE HIGHLANDS
From Peter Graham

You asked me what I thought of the painting
as we stood, rain-damp, in the gallery that day,
having escaped the Manchester weather for an hour.
What I thought of was that evening I trekked
alone up to High Force in the storm to see
the waterfall in spate. The bracken blown flat
by the wind, the sky a blackening bruise.
How I stood above the churning broil
as the water turned itself inside out,
on the edge, with my arms out wide, hoping
to take off - something like that farmer
poised at the end of the shattered bridge,
driving the animals towards safety. Or perhaps,
looking at him again, maybe he too was
teetering on a brink, thinking of jumping in,
of hitting the water, of not even trying to swim.

GAUGING THE FLOOD

At this line nothing can be done
as the white-water wall washes away
tree, stone, everything in the wake
of its spate that rushes down,
down,
down, the clough. The beck has found
its voice, has bulked up, has had enough.
On the valley floor people pack windows, doors
with sandbags, move to higher ground
as the flood swallows streets, houses, shops.
Imperceptibly the water drops.
Objects emerge from their immersion,
like the ruins of lost civilisations.
People return home to learn of loss.
To sweep and wipe and squeege and mop.
Banks upstream are stripped of fern and moss.
New places made between the rocks.
As it drops the beck is still a force
though more discerned in its course
as it calms, no longer in a rush,
recalibrates its static hush, meanders
through gullies, unspools its anger.
In pools above the weir, water clears.

A stone mosaic filters through.
Midges swarm in frantic swirls,
new traceries of fern unfurl,
foxgloves, poppies, viper bugloss.
A small fish leaps with purpose
sending shockwaves out along the surface.

RASPBERRY PICKING AT HIGH FORCE

It is too late in the season now.
Along the woodland verge the greens brown.
The bushes are bare but for a few
shrivelled chandeliers, tiny blood clots
on the canes dark veins. The falls drop.
The river mills, churning the dark slurry
of a dead year. The trees have begun
to seep. Bracken rots in the understorey.
Give it time and the colour will come back,
the raspberries will grow sweet and fat
in these thickets like the tongues
of a choir. The birds will sing again,
transfusing summer into their songs.
Do not worry. It will not be long.

CARTOGRAPHER'S FEAR

It is as though the road
skirts clifftops tonight.
The trees a choropleth of darkness,
as though the ink
of some metaphysical printer
has run dry. Leafless,
they are rivers as seen from space,
branches becoming tributaries,
emptying into the swallowing
estuary of sky. Drowning the stars.

NIGHT HORSES

We rendered the world into existence that night;
not fully formed in the headlights
of the car, but a state of liminal reverberations
that represented hedge, gate, post, tree, sign.
Each one flaring incandescently along the periphery
of the road. Everywhere subsumed by darkness
save the luminary motes of farms across
the moor.
   We rounded the bend and there
they were, not made by any light of ours,
but waiting, five horses stood in the road,
solid and heavy in their own air.
They gathered round the car, luminous
in our glow, liquid in their movements.
We inched through their crowding
as we all eyed each other with the same
sense of wonder,
   at the suddenness
      and brightness
         of being.

CAPACITY FOR JOY

In the early morning dark the headlights
cut a flute of brightness along the road
by Carrick's Haugh. Nothing's lit
but the necessities of tarmac and verge.
The white fence is a running margin
ruling out everything beyond its border,
where shadows deepen to black.
I cannot see them but they are there, watching.
For them the sudden blaze of the car is a comet,
streaking through the void. All day they stand
while I attend to meetings and email purges,
a disappointing lunch, banal conversations.
They crop grass, drink from the reed
tassled pool. They are aware of the deer
in the plantation, the pheasant's erratic announcement
as it chocks through the scrub. They shelter
under the larch during a rain shower.
All of this goes on in my absence. And more.
All unseen but happening none the less,
with no need for validation or prescription.
Returning down the darkening dusk settled road
I see them by the fence. Not waiting for me,
just there, our synchronous habits
bringing us to near spatial and temporal alignment,

as close to understanding as we will ever be.
A comet reverses back along its flightpath,
and three ghosts melt into the rear-view mirror,
back to their darkness. Still there.
Still watching.

ETAL CASTLE

Walking through the gate I flashed back
a decade to that summer day
we rocked up here on our way north,
when everything was fresh and new,
the panorama of our thirties
unrolling across the distance like the Cheviots.

In that moment I half expected to meet
those otherselves, off to Braemar
and that stormy night below Creag Choinnich,
such was the déjà vu
on seeing the keep, the curtain wall,
the shadow-curve of the defensive ditch,

all seemingly the same.
It was as though I had turned for a second
and four-thousand sunrises had passed
over the lawn, the stones,
leaving no trace but the deepened holloways
on the back of my hands.

That evening, down on the weir
we watched a heron standing in the river,
a split-pin lewis perfectly poised
amid the churning spate, its whole machinery
employed with nothing but keeping still.
Slowly the sun dropped beyond the hill.

TETHERED

All I could think about when you told me
That we had lost it, was that night
We spent camping in Braemar
And the wind funnelling down the channel
Between the hills at such a rate
That it bent the tent poles and pushed
The fabric almost into our faces,
As though there were great pressure
Being applied on the outside
And the whole of the world
Was sitting on our refuge, crushing it down.
That crush has come again,
Though different now in the silence
Of the stairs, and the rain is now your sobs
And the wind the startled breaths
You take on my shoulder.
That night I thought that we might blow away.
I could feel the guy ropes burying themselves
Deeper, holding on for dear life,
Knowing that if they weren't tethered
In the ground that they could end up anywhere.
That tugging is you holding onto my shirt,
Pulling it tightly in your stooped sadness,

Holding you up. As though without a firm
Grip you might take off and end up somewhere
Beyond that valley, that field and these stairs.

TRANSVERSE ORIENTATION

Vega declined at 39° - so Columbus knew
that he was north of the equator
west-bound, dead reckoned
by the angle of light thrown down
and the twitching finger of the compass.

*

Around the candle the moth oscillates,
dragged into a highly elliptical orbit
by the fulminating frequencies of light,
a luminescent signal that love
draws, fires, expends.

*

The road signs on the A1
read like roll call:
Wetherby, Richmond, Scotch Corner.
Somewhere in the ember glow of the village
our house lights burn, waiting.

READING LUPERCAL IN ALL SAINTS' LIBRARY

This book has been here longer than my life.
Dust covered, unread in a generation.
The last date stamped 1982.

Braemar freezes.
In San Carlos British soldiers land,
Mary Rose is lifted from her grave.

Thirty years unthumbed.
The pike floats on the water's surface,
its great teeth gone.

Footpaths are weeded over.
Algae scums the surface,
anglers avoid the pools.

Words mould the autumnal leaves.
The gutters stink of biology.

JOHN CLARE'S GREEN COAT

'For I had been measured at the Taylors for a new olive green coat a colour which I had long aimd at.'

After he died they laid it out

        and realised it wasn't a coat but a map.

The woollen green was made of grass,

        the buttons a copse of trees.

Where the cuffs were scuffed and marked

        there were acres of moorland scrub.

The pockets fell into deep dales

        and the lapels were plateau tops.

Someone pulled at a rip in the seam

        at the top of the arm and a scattering

of songbirds ruptured, upwards.

        They followed each thread like a river,

looking for a source, and out of the cave

        of a sleeve rolled a pebble,

                a mountain,

                    the Earth.

HS2

'Saw three fellows at the end of Royce Wood who I found were laying out the plan for an Iron Rail Way from Manchester to London – it is to cross over Round Oak Spring ... I little thought that fresh intrusions would interrupt ... my solitudes after the Inclosure' John Clare June 4th, 1825

Honeysuckle. Squirrels. Hawthorn. Sedge. Hillside. Setts. House-Martins. Sycamores. Hedgerows. Sphagnum. Horse Chestnut. Sparrows. Haughs. Springs. *Hacked. Slashed.* Hatchlings. Sheep. Honey Buzzard. Silver Birch. Hyacinth. Siskin. Hooded Crow. SSSI. Hawfinch. Shoveler. Hazel. Snowdrops. Hen Harrier. Sage. *Hammered. Smashed.* Horseradish. St John's Wort. Hollyhock. Skylark. Hornbeam. Snapdragons. Herring Gull. Sweet Pea. Hydrangea. Serin. *Harmed. Suffered.* Hedgehog. Sand Martin. Hens. Sorrel. Horses. Spiders. Honey Bee. Strawberry. Hornet. Silverfish. Hock. Swallows. Hover Fly. Stoats. Hawkmoth. Sedge Warbler. Hares. Swans. Heron. Snails. High Speed. Homogenised Society. Happening Soon.

SOURCE

We were in Battlefield Cavern at White Scar,
at the end of the tour when the guide
shifted our gaze away from the boulder
blitzed floor to the shell holes in the roof.
'Avens' he said, 'where water has driven
its way through the soft rock creating
a labyrinth of shafts to the surface.'
And I wondered how great the pressure
must have been to push water so violently
through the Earth, straining upwards for escape.
It was months afterwards when I tramped alone
across the moor, pissed off with work and home
to where the Tees bubbled from the ground,
that I finally understood the mechanics
of release, as the weight in my chest
began to decrease, and all those weeks
of being so highly strung dispelled out
in a yell at the top of my lungs.

STAITHES

Down the steep bank into history
the cottages are primed in their sunset colours,
each name echoing something long lost;
Felicity, Shangri-la, Confidence.
Narrow ginnels run like tributaries
to the converted workshops and yards,
where the sailmakers, boat-builders, fishermen,
have been replaced by souvenir shops and cafes.

In the harbour a single flat-bottomed coble
sloshes idly in the slack water.
Tourists line up outside the convenience
as though it were a customshouse.
No signs now of the barrels of piss
ferried in from London for the dyeing trade,
but the alum quarries cratering the cliffs
still bear their lunar scars two centuries on.

Dusk swells to darkness but no lights are raised
in the empty rooms of Captain Cook's holiday let,
from whose windows a boy once looked out
and saw beyond the lobster pots and slimy walls,
beyond the catch and the contraband cargoes of tea,

to where the gun-metal sea unrolled itself like a map,
and the blank and weatherless horizons
promised adventure, discovery.

FROZEN POOL IN HOTBURN PLANTATION

Dead eye of the earth, what do you see
through your cataract.

The ground mimics you
in its bridal dress.

Something has pierced your veil,
shattering your illusion.

Did it escape, or is it there now
until the thaw.

You are cracking up:
contour lines map collisions.

Something moves within your womb.
You are not so pure,

something dark
against the whiteness stirs.

THOUGHTS ON AN AFTERMATH

In the long grass by the lane I found a doe
crumpled into a question mark.
It had been there a while, its hide cured
to a thin and hollow drum.
Then a fawn tucked in tightly by its side,
as just as papery and empty in the eyes.
I turned back home; my Sunday spoiled
by that aftermath and later, worse,
the thoughts of which of the two
I hoped had gone first.

FALLEN

It has been a skeleton in the hedge
For a while. No leaves this spring, just its bare
Bones starkly white against the dark foliage
Of the hawthorn and beech. Now it's there,
Fallen in the garden, wind-wrecked, spread
Wide like the filigree of a shattered crown.
We have become as reverent as for our own dead,
And we let it lie for days in state upon its ground,
Touching the earth, at last, where its shadow once reached.
And we will learn to wait in the long days of summer to come,
For other things to move in to fill the breach
Of its absence, like nettles, foxgloves, and the sun.

GONE TO SEED

The old shed was half-hidden underneath
a tarpaulin of leaves and a scaffold
of low hanging branches, so it could barely
be seen from the lane. I squeezed through the gap
in the gate, its swing stoppered by silt, ballast
dumped by the burn in last year's flood.
Inside were a few oil drums, rolls of barbed wire,
and an old tractor that had been left to rust.
I climbed into the cab, the seat a sphagnum sponge,
the instrument panel a secret nook of dust.
It must have sat there for years, unmoved,
as the sunlight traced the seasons on the wall,
simply left after one last harvest or plough
by someone who was not coming back for it now.

LIFE STUDY
St. Peyronis

All day I lay beneath the walnut,
indolent in the heavy heat of the meadow.
Nothing moved in the breathless air
besides butterflies buffering between flowers
and wasps prospecting the cave of a Coke can.
A woodpecker tapped, pigeons cooed,
a jay screeched like a prehistoric thing,
and the sky remained an undived pool.
That was life uncoupled from Time,
where everything happened somewhere else,
and responsibilities were left waiting or lost
in the stillness of a summer's day,
where only the woods anticipated darkness,
their foliage, their slow shadows spreading.

INTO THE DISTANCE

We were coming down through the woods at Gibside
and you were telling me about your drawing,
how you were learning all about perspectives,
how vanishing points represent the place
on the horizon where all parallel lines diminish,
how they angle in together until they intersect
and everything is pulled into one space.
When we reached the path you showed me what you meant,
how the treeline curved into the grey stone
of the track which bent around the grassy bank
until nothing was discernible.
And now, standing here again, without you,
all your lines have finally drawn together
into your own receding, and the memories of you
are nothing more than a replay of that moment's
altered perception, these woods and the grass
and this path stretching into an unfathomable distance,
I think I finally understand.

LOOKING OUT ON THE MENAI STRAIT

The viewpoint is deserted.
The sky a pastel chart.

This age has brought me to the sea,
to this black gorge.

The glaciers are gone but the air is deathly still,
each breath forming new apparitions.

Down amongst the swelling call,
the rocks appear and vanish like humpbacks.

Car headlights glare intermittently,
searchlights arcing.

Soon nothing will be seen
but the moonlit door in the open water.

ANOTHER PLACE

They stand on the beach, waiting.
Looking far out into the horizon
As though, in their stillness, stating
That something is coming to heighten
Their existence. Days, weeks, years
Have passed and still they remain, vigilant
In their watch, ignoring those nagging fears
That their time will pass without incident.
Maybe they are the same as us, thrust
Into a landscape, pinioned into the ground
With no choice but to stand and rust
And wait for the tide to come and drown.

A VIEW OF THE BEACH AT NEWBIGGIN

       graveyard
dried cartilage cracking underfoot
       torsos of driftwood
shells breakers algae
       green phlegm hacked up
rock pools fingerprinted by the wind
       sand   infinitesimal decay
of mountains   a dead crab's
       shucked off armour
footprints cross paths   desire lines
       crows black oil slick rainbow
waves unrolling continental backstory
       broken concrete bunkers
turbines mixing weather fronts
       empty holiday lets gaze vacantly
out   haze light   flatline
       horizon   heavy steel
silhouette   dock yards distant
       sun catching water
incandescent   flashbulbs
       dazzle of distress flares

SITTING ON ROCKS BY PENVEEN LIGHTHOUSE

The chimneys of the mines stalk the horizon.
Drizzle grey in this light, opaque in the last
of the day. Seagulls barred against the wind,
carrier bags caught in an updraft.
The sea rips rough against the rocks,
slapping high white waves that look
like beads pulled from a chain.
Far out, almost out of sight, a boat appears,
vanishes – light sodden in the tin vast gloom.
Its searchlight melts in the mist,
looking for a coupling from the cliffs
where the great gleam of the lighthouse
beckons back, trying to pull it in.

FIGURING IT OUT

She asked me whether I thought that in reality
maths was a better tool to use than poetry
                              to define, with clarity,
the world in which we live. She used the decimal
to make her point, that it can break down data
into its smallest components, offering a level
of comparison that no word could.
                              Fair enough I said,
but tell me how that describes the gradients
of colour in an autumn wood, that no graph
or chart could ever get to the heart of that.
                              She countered
by asking whether any word could accurately
state the true distance of a star. All I could come
up with was that they're pretty far.
                              We argued about
angles, whether knowing that the horizon
was at a certain degree made it any more profound
when watching the sun rise over the sea,
whether knowing the circumference of the whole
meant that you understood the intricacies
of integers.
                              I thought I had her when I asked her

to accurately account in numbers for an abstract
such as Love. She replied,

                      laughing, that that was easy,
that in numeric terms Love equalled two.
And how would you describe it in a sentence
she asked, thinking she'd won.

        But I wasn't done, though I had to agree
that Love in words was also two,

            a couplet bound in a noun phrase,

                      me & you.

POST BOX ON CORPORATION STREET
For Manchester

I have held your names in my mouth,
Swallowed your words, your secrets.
I've kept them inside my armour,
Ready for deliverance. I have shared
Your love, your loss, your joy and pain.
I know your language and if I could talk
I would tell you that I know what it is like
To stand in the rubble of an aftermath;
To breathe in fire and smoke
And feel your insides crackle with fear.
Dust-blind and bang-deaf I have stood
As the city has fallen about me.
But I am here; chipped and scarred.
Let us carry our wounds like stamps of honour.

ACKNOWLEDGEMENTS

With thanks to: Acumen; Allegro; Bad Lilies; Envoi; Honest Ulsterman; Ink, Sweat and Tears; Poetry Village; Sarasvati; Under the Radar and Words for the Wild, where some of these poems first appeared.

'Raspberry Picking at High Force' was first published in the 'After Sylvia' publication from Nine Arches Press as a commended poem.

'Between Little and Great Dun Fell' won the 2024 Mountaineering Scotland Poetry Prize.

'HS2' and 'Cubbington Pear' first appeared in *Footprints Ecopoetry Anthology* from Broken Sleep.

LAY OUT YOUR UNREST